SETTING UP

RODS & LINES

Small Streams: 7½ to 8½ft, #4 to #5.
Larger Streams: 8½ to 9½ft, #6 to #7.
Floating lines are the preferred choice in most situations-deeper water can be searched with wet flies using longer leaders. There are circumstances where a spare spool with a sink-tip, or a sinking line and short leader will pay off.

LEADERS

KNOTLESS TAPERED LEADER: These are available in a variety of lengths and tippet thickness.

COMPOUND: Different fishing conditions and changing situations sometimes require features unobtainable in commercial leaders. Many anglers make up 'compound' or customised leaders from monofilament of varying diameters and lengths.

MATCHING LEADERS TO FLIES

Your leader and tippet should suit both your fly line and the size of flies you plan to use.

	BUTT DIAM (In.)	TIP DIAM (In.)	SIZE	HOOK
10lb.	.026	.011	0X	1/0-6
9lb.	.022	.010	1X	2-6
7lb.	.022	.009	2X	2-6
6lb.	.022	.008	3X	4-10
5lb.	.022	.007	4X	6-14
4lb.	.022	.006	5X	10-18
3lb.	.020	.005	6X	14-22

COMPOUND LEADERS

Approx 12-15 ft 5x All Purpose Dry Fly Leader

.017	.015	.013	.011	.009	.008	.007	.006
12"	20"	20"	20"	14"	14"	18"	26"-60"

Approx 10-12 ft 4x All Purpose Nymphing Leader

.021	.019	.017	.015	.013	.011	.009	.007
40"	16"	14"	8"	8"	8"	8"	24"-36"

Approx 6-7 ft All Purpose Wet Fly Leader

.45	.40	.35	.30	.24	.018
24"	17"	6"	6"	6"	20-26"

KNOTS & RIGS

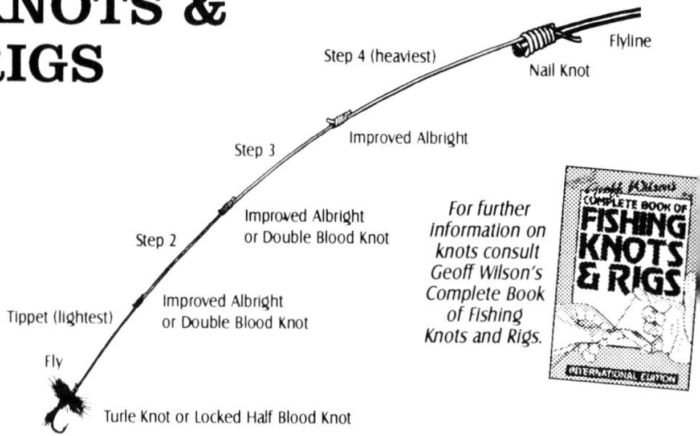

For further information on knots consult Geoff Wilson's Complete Book of Fishing Knots and Rigs.

ATTACHING FLIES TO LEADER

Locked Half Blood Knot

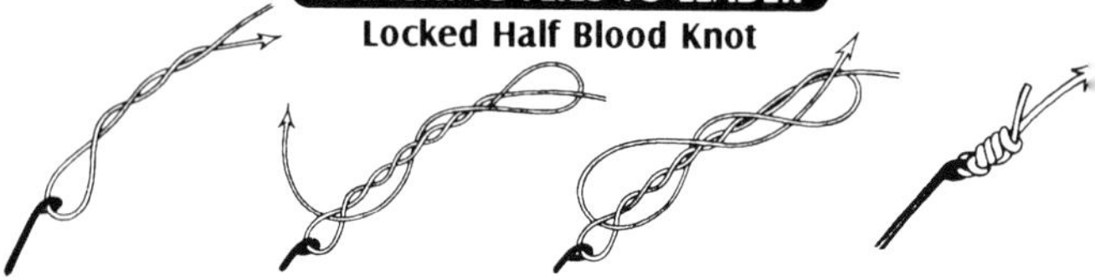

1. Thread the eye of the hook and wind the tag back around the main line four or five times.
2. Wind the tag back around the knot and through the eye of the first wrap of line around the eye of the hook.
3. Now thread the tag back through the loop at the top of the knot. This locks the knot so it can't slip.
4. Tighten the knot wi gentle pressure on th tippet.

Improved Turle Knot

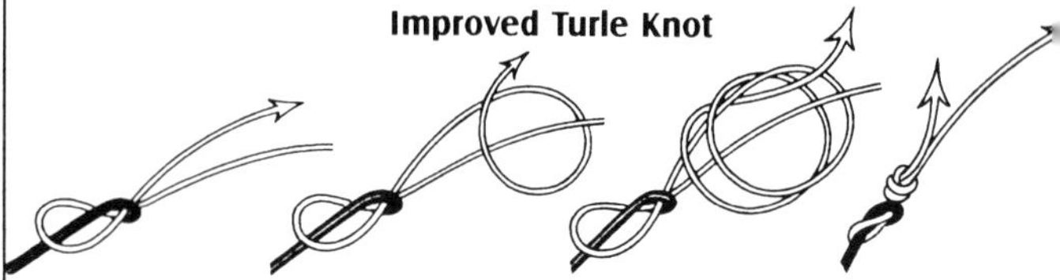

1. Thread the line through hook eye, take the line around the head of the fly and back through the eye of the hook again.
2. Encircle the standing part of the tippet with the tag.
3. And again, making two turns in all, then pass the tag over, and back through the centre of those two turns.
4. Close up the knot wit gentle pressure on th tag and slide the knc right down into the ey of the hook.

ATTACHING FLYLINE TO LEADER

Nail Knot

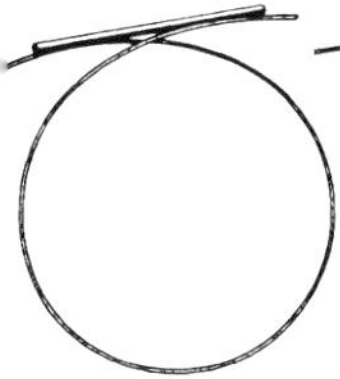

1. Make a loop in the backing or leader and lay the metal tube alongside the cross-over.

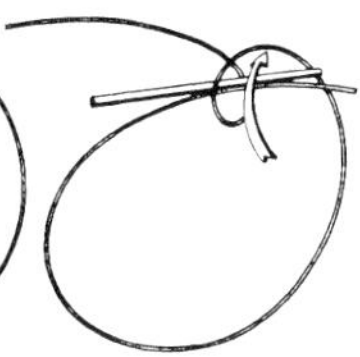

2. Begin wrapping the tube with the backing or leader.

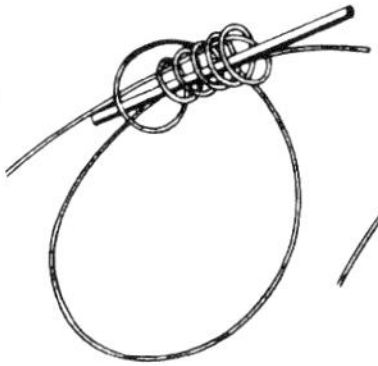

3. Make at least six wraps.

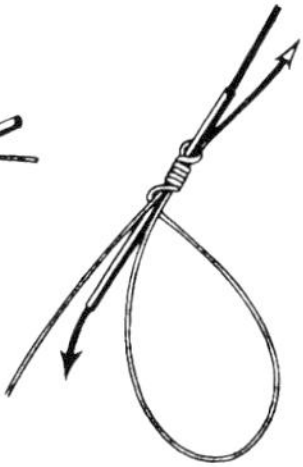

4. Close the knot up tight on the tube and insert the fly line into the tube.

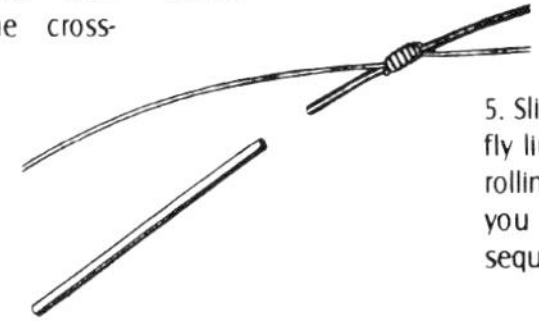

5. Slide the knot off the tube, onto the fly line, and close the knot up gently, rolling it between thumb and finger as you do so to keep the wraps in sequence.

JOINING LEADER SECTIONS

Improved Albright Knot

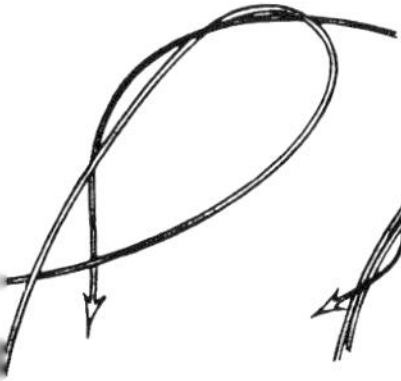

1. Make a loop in the heavier line and pass the lighter line through the loop.

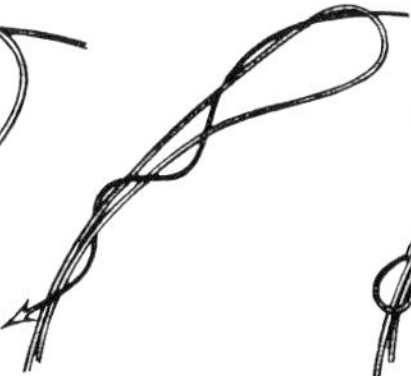

2. Bind the lighter line around the loop of heavier line five times.

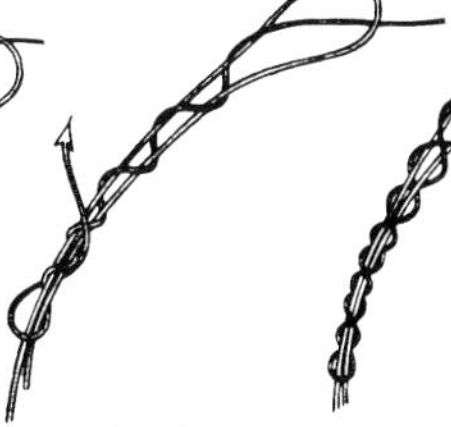

3. Then bind five times back in the opposite direction.

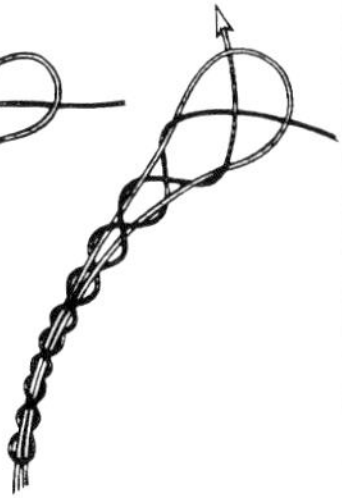

4. Here we have five wraps of line one direction around the loop and five in the opposite direction.

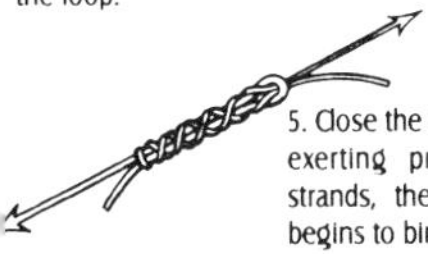

5. Close the knot up gently, first by exerting pressure on all four strands, then – when the knot begins to bind – release both tags and tension the knot as shown.

6. The finished knot should look like this.

FISH FACTORS

RAINBOW TROUT

A hardy, streamlined species renowned for their fighting qualities. They favour cold, fast, aerated waters and are opportunistic, rapacious feeders that will actively chase down food and readily take a fly.

BROWN TROUT

A wary, fiercely territorial fish that prefer calm to moderate flowing sections of a river. They often become infrequent, nocturnal feeders with age.

WATER TEMPERATURE AND OXYGEN REGIMES

Important factors to consider when determining the quality of the fishing. The ideal temperature ranges are:
Rainbow Trout 12-15°C (55-60°F)
Brown Trout 13-21°C (50-70°F)

Trout cannot tolerate the lack of dissolved oxygen in warm water, therefore, when temperatures become extreme, trout will react by:

- Becoming totally non responsive to conserve their energy.
- Moving into cooler, aerated water i.e. riffles, pocket wate below in-flowing feeder stream
- Shifting from the body of a poo to the aerated headwaters.
- Remaining in the deepes coolest or shadiest part of a poo until conditions improve.

BAROMETRIC PRESSURE

Some anglers argue that thi affects fish (and insects) activity and that fishing is poor on falling barometer and best as i rises. However, many dispute thi and have done well unde 'unfavourable conditions.

ANGLING PRESSURE

Heaviest on easily accessibl waters on public holidays an weekends. To avoid the crowds try walking for at least 30 minute from any of the main acces points to increase your chances o finding an undisturbed stretch o water.

Tip: Customised leaders can pick up algae on their joining knots-try coating these knots with glue.

PRIME TROUT LIES

River trout favour lies that combine:
• Protection • Minimal current • Good food supply

DEPRESSIONS

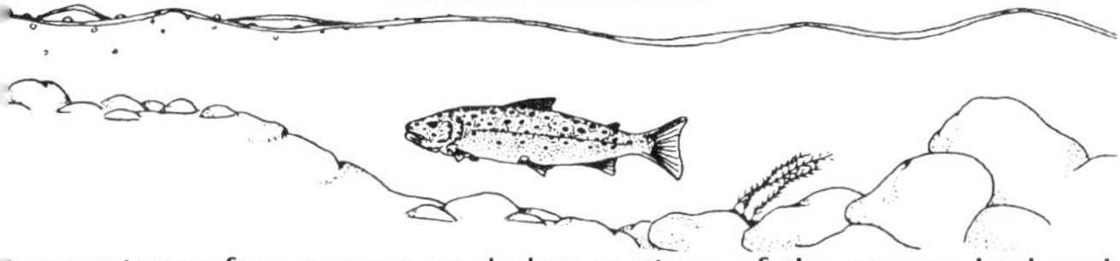

)epressions often appear as darker sections of the stream bed and ›ffer trout a current breaking lie. ***Holding and feeding lie.***

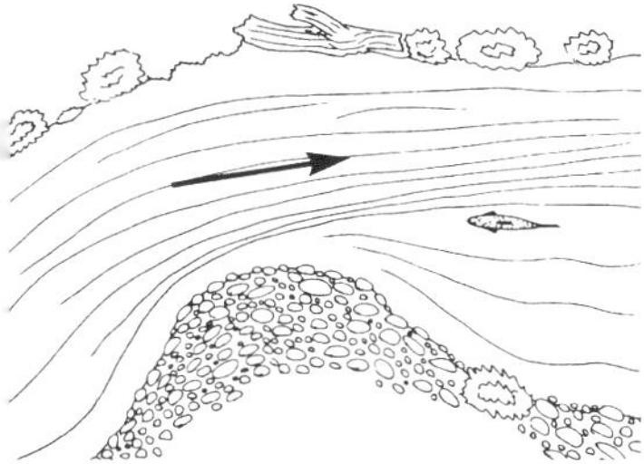

SEAMS

Seams are formed where currents of varying speeds or direction, converge. Trout hold in the slower water and leisurely intercept food as it drifts by in the faster current. ***Holding and feeding lie.***

EYES

:yes are the calm, often triangular ,ections of water found on :ither side of headwater currents. ***-eeding and occasional holding 'ies.***

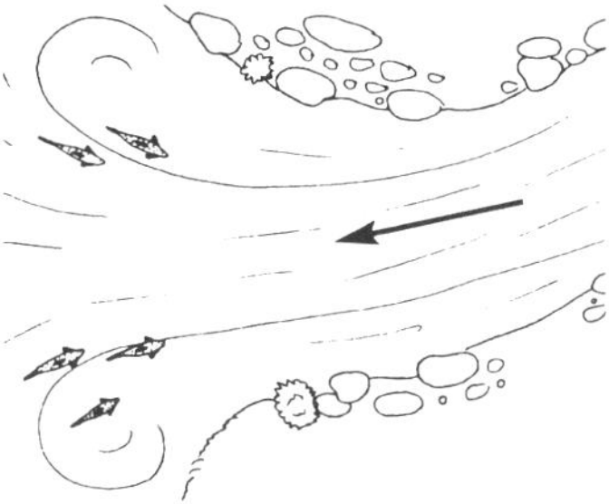

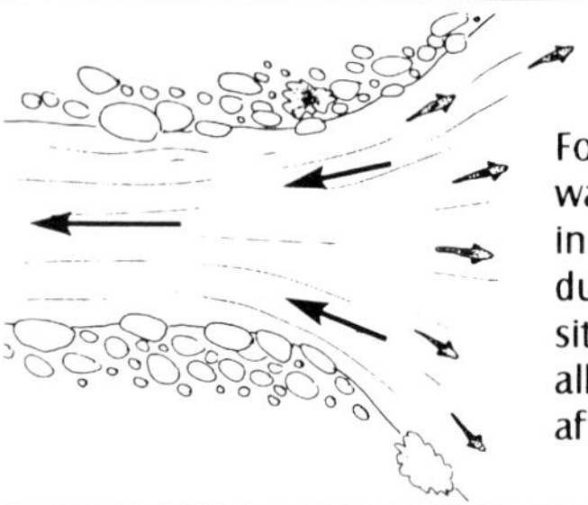

TAILOUTS

Food is concentrated in the shallo water, forming productive feeding lie in the low light conditions of daw dusk and through the night. Trout wi sit in mid to top water actively feedin all day in colder months and lat afternoon in summer. ***Feeding lie.***

STREAM BED

Fish often hold on the bottom where the river hydraulics offer a cushion of relatively calm water. ***Holding lie, occasionally feeding from here.***

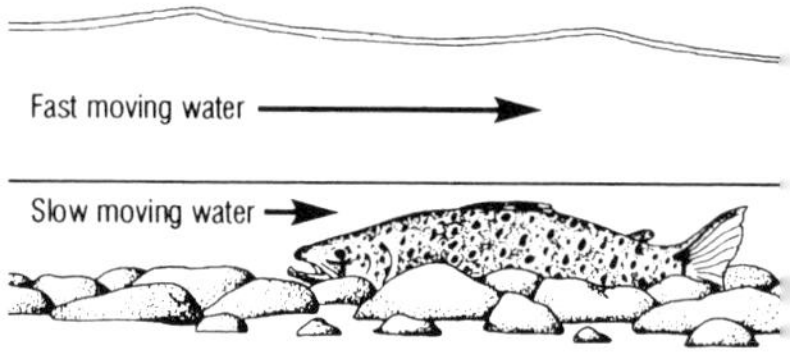

OVERHANGING TREES & FOLIAGE

These offer shade, protectiv cover and a source o terrestrial food.
Opportunistic feeding lie.

UNDERCUT BANKS

A favoured lie for brown trout. These occur where erosive currents scour out the bank wall below the surface, forming a food channelling cavity. ***Holding and feeding lies, especially when the river is in flood.***

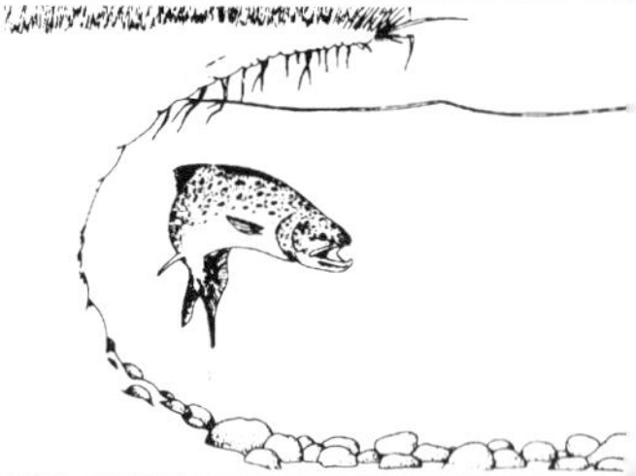

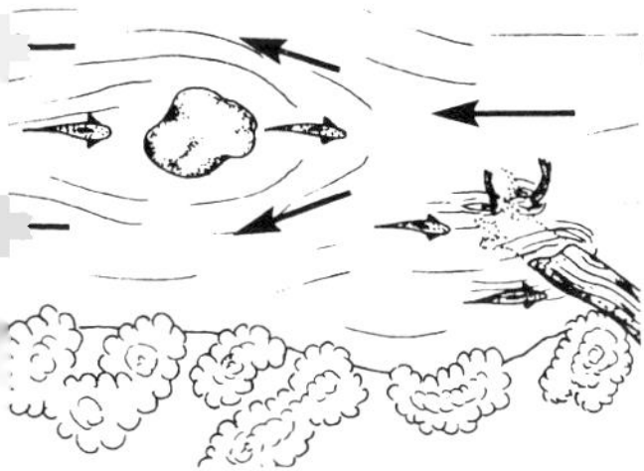

STRUCTURE/OBSTRUCTIONS

Trout can hold in the hydraulic cushion in front, behind or on each side of any obstruction that breaks the current if the lie is deep enough. Boils and swirls often pinpoint subsurface obstructions. ***Holding and feeding lies.***

WEED BEDS

These offer trout protective cover and a readily abundant food supply. Trout will often hold or cruise in the clear pockets amongst the weed. ***Feeding lies.***

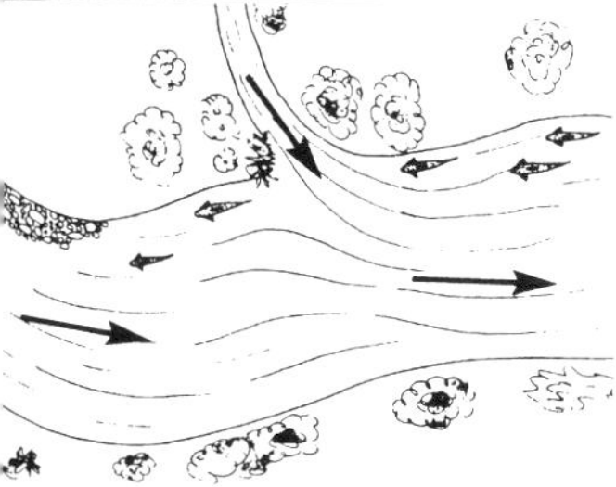

INFLOWING CREEKS

Trout congregate below the mouth of tributaries to feed and, during warm conditions, take advantage of the cool waters these streams often provide. ***Feeding lies.***

BUBBLE LINES

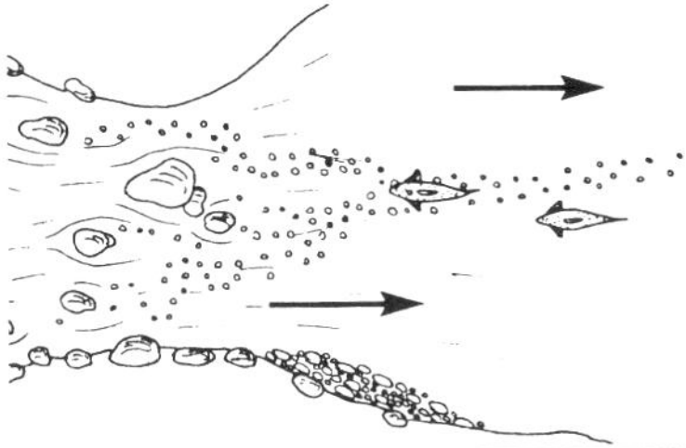

The bubbles ride on the surface of the water following the course of the current. Trout congregate under or in their vicinity to capitalise on the food items the current carries. ***Feeding lie, short term holding lie.***

SECTION FOUR

DRY FLY TECHNIQUES

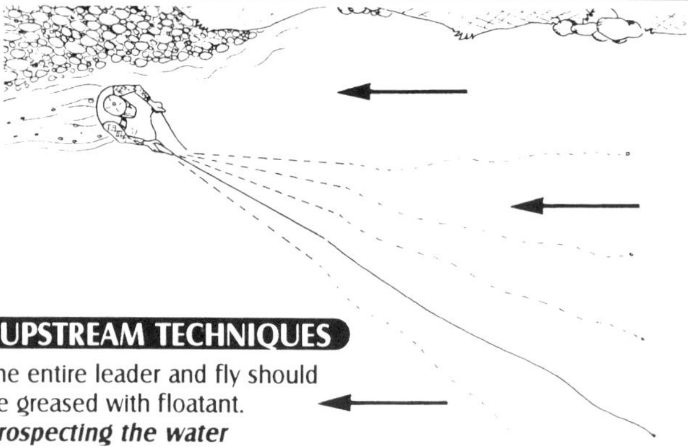

UPSTREAM TECHNIQUES

The entire leader and fly should be greased with floatant.

Prospecting the water

- Execute a standard cast of 20-40 ft on a slight angle upstream. Keep pace with the fly by gathering the slack line off the water as it drifts back towards you.
- Work your casts across a parallel 'front' of water placing the fly 1-3 ft along from the previous cast, covering any suspected or obvious lies.
- Move forward 10-15 ft and repeat the process. Your fly will be constantly exploring new water.

Targeting feeding fish

- Ideally try to position yourself so that only a short, accurate cast is required. Long casts can be inaccurate and subject to unseen drag.
- Try a practice cast to one side of the fish to ascertain the required amount of flyline needed so that your first presentation is on target.
- The fly should be placed gently on a slight angle at least 3-5 ft ahead of the trout and allowed to drift down over the lie. If the fly is not taken, let it drift well clear of the trout before gently lifting it off the water to recast.
- Unless the fish has clearly rejected the pattern or stopped rising altogether, allow at least 10 drifts before changing the fly or tippet diameter.

DOWNSTREAM TECHNIQUES

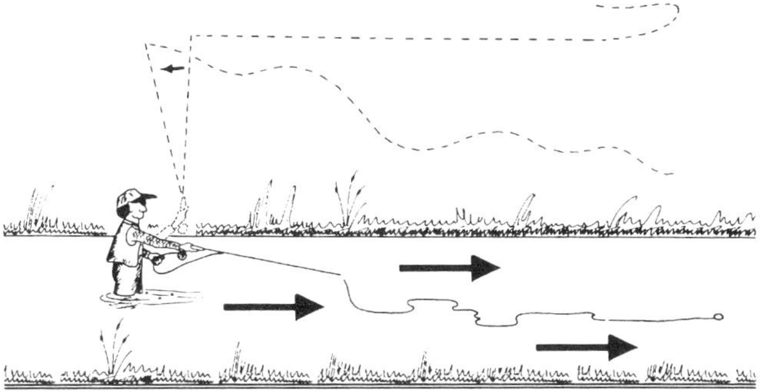

Parachute cast:

- False cast for a normal presentation but feed out more line than is required to reach the fish.
- On the delivery cast aim the line high and as your arm reaches the 12 o'clock position, stop!
- As the line straightens in front of you, sharply jerk the rod back to 1 o'clock and then allow the line to land on the water.
- The slack line should drift downstream behind the fly. To increase the drift simply feed out more line.

Wiggle/'S' cast:

- When powering into the forward stroke aim the cast high and release a little extra line as the cast unrolls. At this point wiggle the rod from side to side.
- Wiggling early in the cast produces curves at the end of the line whilst wiggling late will provide curves nearer the rod tip.
- Wiggle and feed line out to increase the drift.

MENDING LINE

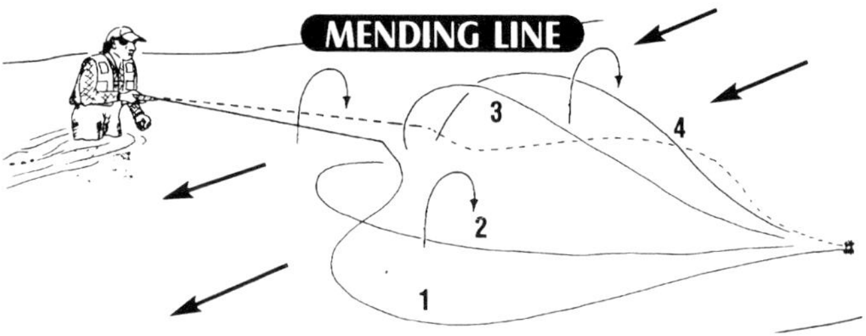

The angler must develop line mending skills to nullify the effects of drag. The most common method involves flicking a roll of slack line upstream against the current.

- Draw in slack line between the rod tip and the downstream 'belly' in the line.
- Lower the rod tip to water level and aim it at the 'belly'.
- Roll the rod forcefully in an arc upstream whilst simultaneously releasing a small amount of line.
- This motion creates an upstream 'belly' and allows a longer drag free drift.
- Floating lines allow this process to be repeated as often as required.

CROSS STREAM TECHNIQUE

The Reach Cast is ideal for casting over conflicting currents because it will place the flyline upstream of the fly and allow a drag free drift.

Reach Cast: *(right)*

- Power the rod with a normal casting stroke in the direction the fly is to go.
- As the line shoots forward in the delivery stroke, reach the rod as far as you can upstream. The flyline will land upstream on an angle from the fly.
- Track the drift with the rod tip.
- Once the fly starts drifting, constantly mend line to prevent drag.

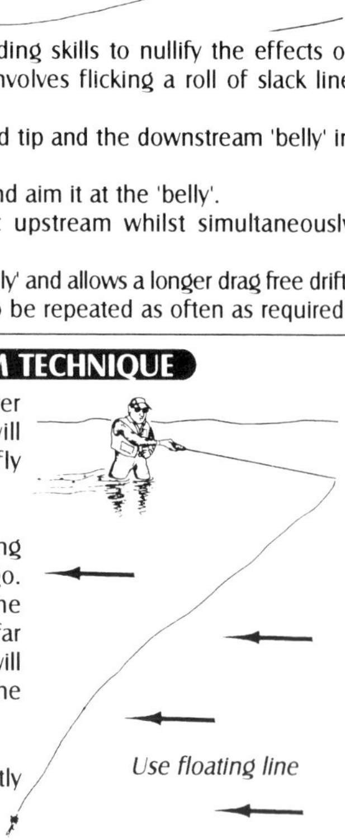

DRAG

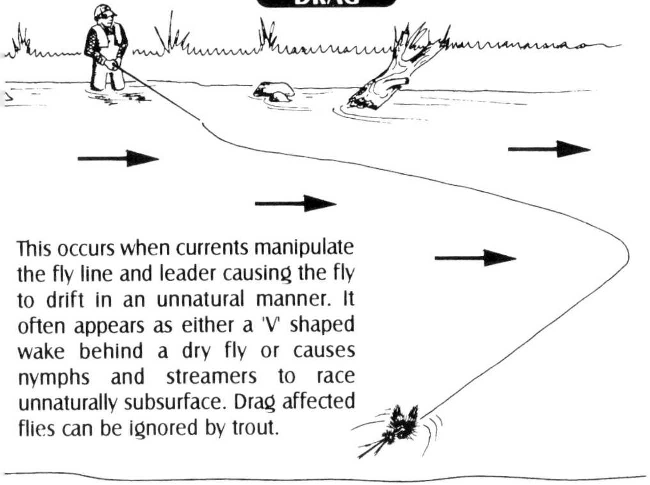

This occurs when currents manipulate the fly line and leader causing the fly to drift in an unnatural manner. It often appears as either a 'V' shaped wake behind a dry fly or causes nymphs and streamers to race unnaturally subsurface. Drag affected flies can be ignored by trout.

MECHANICS OF TROUT RISE

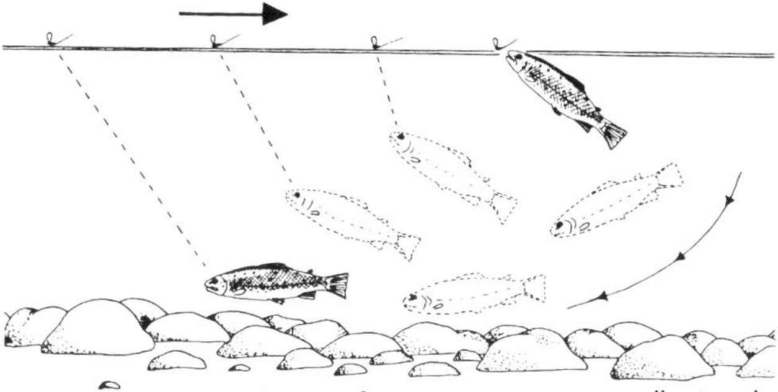

Surface feeding in medium to fast water a trout generally rises by drifting downstream until it is directly under the fly. After either taking or rejecting it the fish returns to the bottom and swims back up to its lie.

SECTION FIVE

NYMPHING TECHNIQUES

UPSTREAM, ACROSS AND MEND

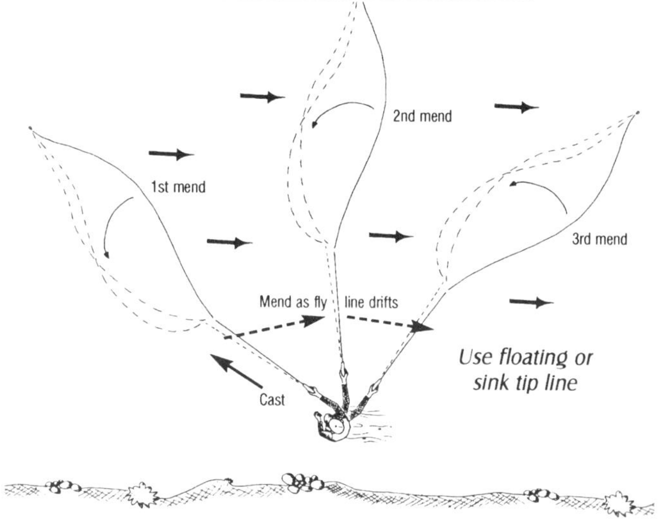

An effective method if trout are taking emergers.

- Cast the fly on an angle upstream and across, immediately instigate an upstream mend.
- **This technique can be used with or without a strike indicator.**
- Flies do not generally sink deeply so weighted/bead head patterns or split shot may be required.
- Trout often strike as the line swings across the current raising the imitation enticingly toward the surface like an emerger.
- Before recasting, give the line a few short strips.

UPSTREAM TECHNIQUE

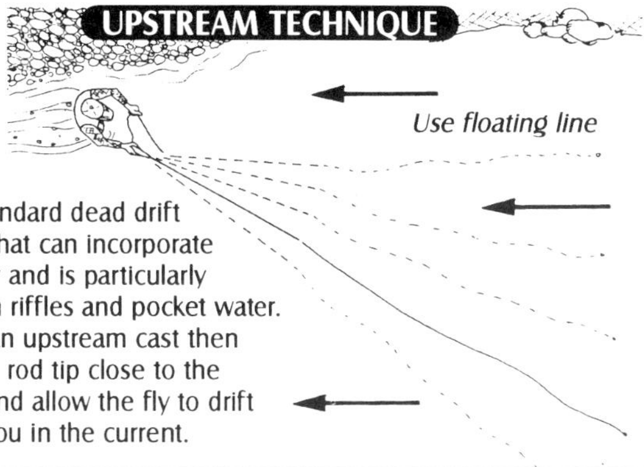

This is a standard dead drift technique that can incorporate an indicator and is particularly effective on riffles and pocket water.

- Execute an upstream cast then lower the rod tip close to the surface and allow the fly to drift back to you in the current.

STRIKE INDICATORS

These are highly visible floating materials, like wool or plastic foam, attached to leaders to provide a visual cue of a strike by pausing, being dragged under or deviating across the flow. A good attachment point is around twice the depth of the water.

Tip - SEARCHING WATER

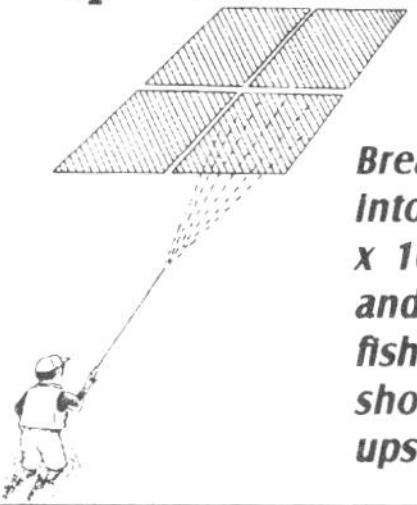

Break the water up into imaginary 10 x 10 foot squares and systematically fish each grid with short 15-30 foot upstream casts.

SECTION SIX

STREAMERS

Streamers are typically large, bulky flies that make excellent search patterns, particularly when water levels are high and discoloured. Experiment with fishing depth, retrieval speed and the type of fly used - the correct combination of all three will catch fish.

DOWN & ACROSS SWING

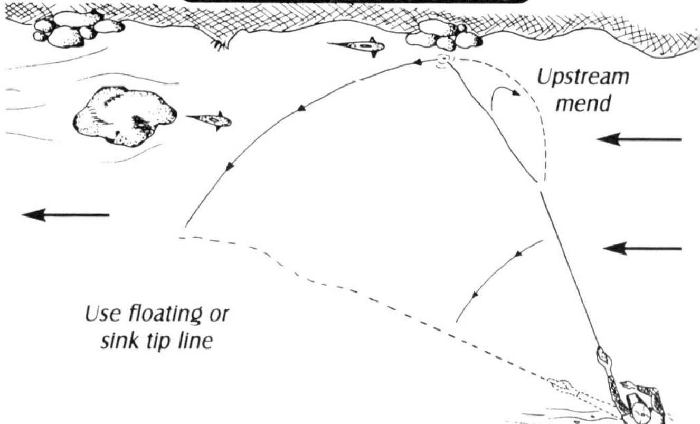

This method systematically explores the water and will present the fly to a large number of fish.

- Cast on an angle downstream and quickly throw an upstream menc to slow the drift and allow the fly to sink. A weighted pattern or spli shot directly above the fly may help.
- Hold the rod tip close to the water allowing the line to slowly draw the fly in an arc across the current. If you feel the fly is moving too quickly throw another upstream mend.

- Manipulate the line of drift with the rod tip to work the fly through and around any potential lies.
- When the line straightens below you, give the fly a few tantalising strips.

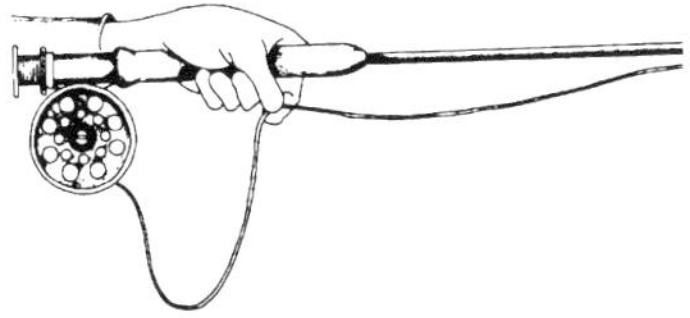

- Trout can take streamers violently so keep a section of slack line off the reel to act as a shock absorber.
- Take a few steps downstream and repeat the process.

BACKWATER PRESENTATION

This is a productive technique to use in large pools or backwaters when fish are holding on the bottom or cruising.

- Cast straight out but slightly upstream and allow the fly plenty of time to sink to the bottom.
- A slow hand twist, short strip or dead slow retrieve is usually productive.

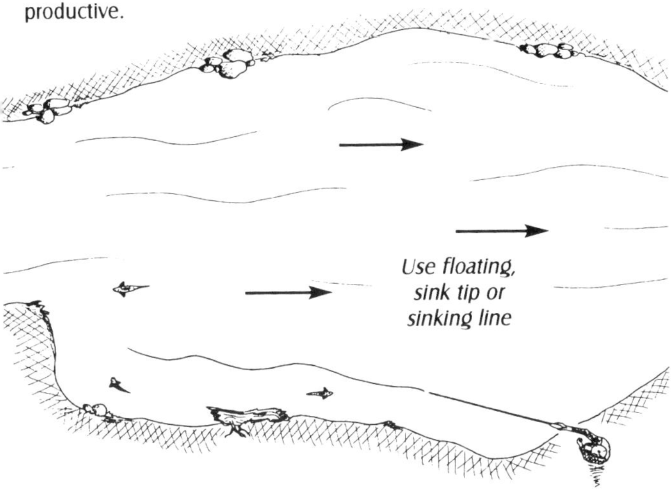

ADVANCED CASTING TECHNIQUES

CURVE CAST

Requires practice but it is a very useful technique to master, particularly when casting around obstacles in the current.

- The rod is angled 45 deg away from the body during the casting motion.
- Overpower the presentation cast and as the line straightens out it will be jerked back causing the leader to form a right hand curve.

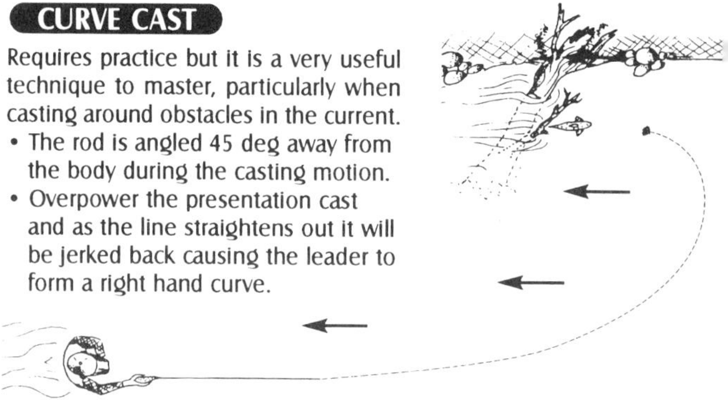

TUCK CAST

Useful when nymphing in fast flowing water where only short drag free drifts are possible. This technique allows the fly to land first.

- Aim the line at about head height above the water. The forward cast is stopped abruptly at the 10 o'clock position and the rod jerked back crisply to 11 o'clock.
- As the fly falls directly downward into the water, lower your rod tip.

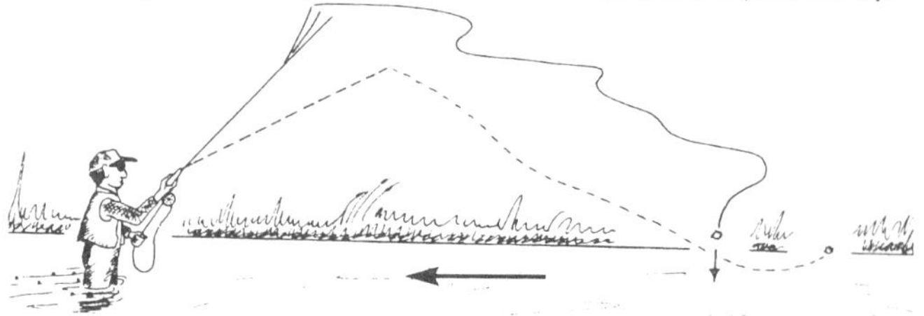

ROLL CAST

An excellent option when back casts cannot be executed whilst casting in the wind or when nymphing in riffles. Works best with a floating line.

- Peel off approximately 30 ft of line onto the water in front of you.
- Smoothly raise the rod to the 1 o'clock position. Your rod hand should be about head height.
- Slightly angle the rod away from your body, with the line hanging on the outside of the rod and slightly behind you. Pause.
- Aim the cast to the left of the line on the water and drive the rod forward with a sharp, crisp power stroke stopping abruptly at the 11 o'clock position.
    - The line should roll out in an oval shape until it straightens to present the fly.

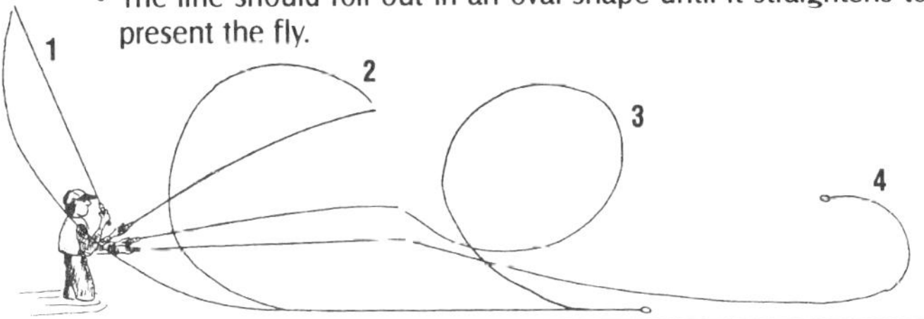

PILE CAST

An effective upstream cast when fast water is flowing between you and the fish.

- Aim the forward cast at about head height. As the line unrolls, drop the rod tip to the water.
- The forward section of the line and leader will collapse limply onto the water, in a heap, providing plenty of slack line to offer a drag free drift over the fish.

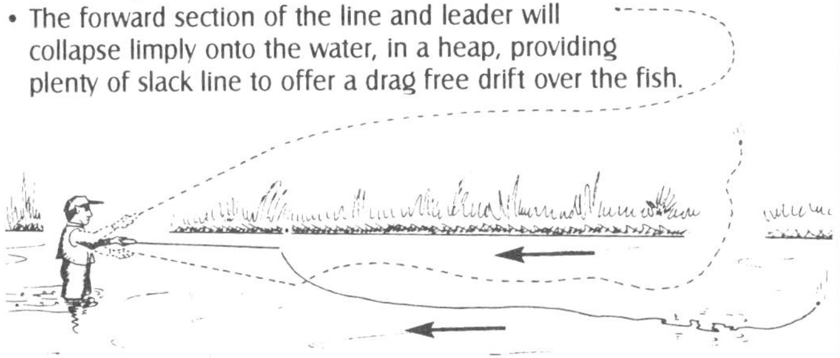

SECTION EIGHT

WATER TYPES & FISHING METHODS

RIFFLES

Fast flowing, aerated sections of a river that typically rise a few inches up to four feet or more and have a choppy, turbulent surface. The oxygenated water harbours a large percentage of a stream's nymph population whilst sunlight encourages weed and plant growth. This combination makes riffles the principle food producing region of a stream and a favourite location for fish during warm weather. Common aquatic insects are **mayfly nymphs, caddis larvae** and (in some areas) **stonefly nymphs.**

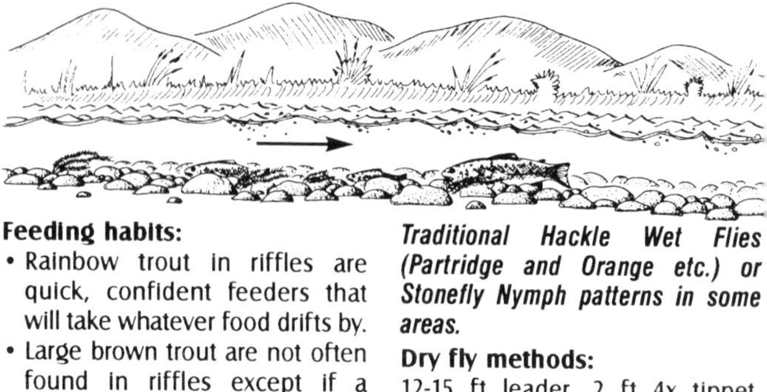

Feeding habits:

- Rainbow trout in riffles are quick, confident feeders that will take whatever food drifts by.
- Large brown trout are not often found in riffles except if a substantial hatch is in progress.

Nymphing methods:

9 ft leader, 2-3 ft 4x tippet. Upstream indicator nymphing is best.

Flies:

Size 10-16 ***Small Fur-bodied Nymphs (Hare, Seal's Fur or substitutes), Traditional Hackle Wet Flies (Partridge and Orange etc.) or Stonefly Nymph patterns in some areas.***

Dry fly methods:

12-15 ft leader, 2 ft 4x tippet. Upstream dry fly drift.

Flies:

Size 10-12-14 ***Royal Wulff, Elk Hair Caddis, Adams, Red Tag, Rat-faced McDougal, Humpy, Stimulator, Bogong Beauty.***

POCKET WATER

Where swift currents on steep gradients are interrupted by numerous large rocks, boulders or other prominent structures. Cushions of calm water behind and in front of these current deflecting obstructions provide trout with low energy lies. Common insects are **mayfly nymphs, stonefly nymphs** and **pebble cased caddis larvae.** In some areas **beetles, ants** and **grasshoppers** (if in season) are also taken.

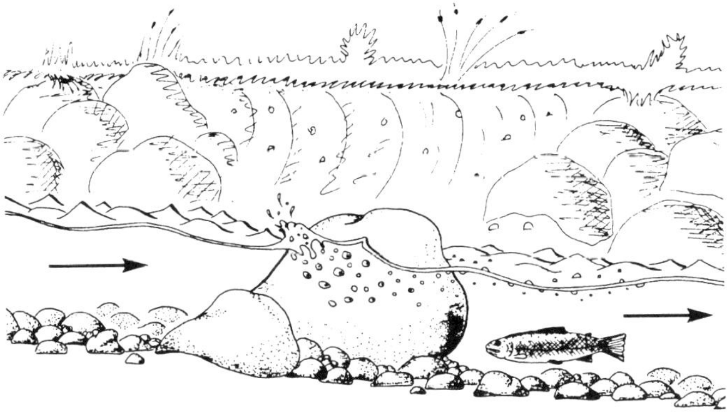

Feeding habits

- Trout in pocket water are generally opportunistic, aggressive feeders.

Nymphing methods:

9 ft leader, 2-3 ft 4x tippet.

Nymphs should be weighted to get them down quickly. Indicator nymphing is useful.

Flies:

Size 10-16 ***Small Fur-bodied Nymphs (Hare, Seal's Fur or substitutes), Traditional Hackle Wet Flies (Partridge and Orange etc.) or Stonefly Nymph patterns in some areas.***

Dry fly methods:

9 ft leader, 2-3 ft 4x tippet.

This type of water requires short distance casts of 25-30 feet or less, using large well-hackled prospecting patterns. Small bodied flies tend to quickly drown in the turbulent water.

Flies:

Size 10-12-14 ***Royal Wulff, Elk Hair Caddis, Adams, Red Tag, Rat-faced McDougal, Humpy, Stimulator, Bogong Beauty.***

RUNS

Characterised by strong, uniform flows that have a mostly smooth surface and a reasonably consistent depth. Fish feel secure from predators in runs and capitalise on food that is washed down from fertile waters upstream. Common species include **caddis larvae (free swimming & case builders), mayfly nymphs** and **stonefly nymphs.** Small **freshwater crayfish** are also eaten if available.

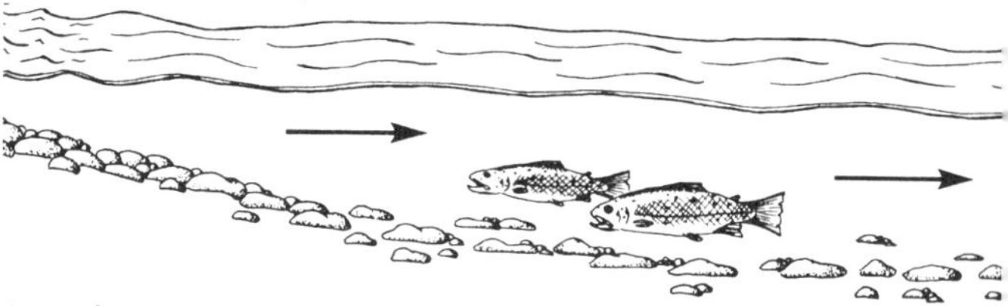

Nymphing methods:

• **Floating line,** 9-12 ft leader, 2-3 ft 3x, 4x tippet.

• **Sinktip line,** 4-6 ft leader, No tippet.

Deep, quick flowing runs are often unproductive nymphing waters due to the difficulty in detecting strikes and getting the flies deep enough. Methodically fish all the prime lies of slower, shallow runs.

Flies:

Size 10-16 ***Hare & Copper, Pheasant Tail, Seals Fur, Stonefly Patterns, Montana Nymph, Prince Nymph, Carrot Nymph, Bird's Nest, Fledermaus, Gray or Red Squirrel Nymphs, Muskrat Nymph.***

Dry fly methods:

9 ft leader, 2-3 ft 5x, 6x tippet. Deep, quick flowing runs generally make poor dry fly waters; fish will rarely expend energy travelling up through the current for a 'small bite'. Drifting flies over prime lies in slower, shallower runs 4 ft deep or less is generally more productive.

Flies:

Size 10-12-14 ***Royal Wulff, Royal Humpy, Elk Hair Caddis, Goddard Caddis, Adams, Stimulator, Hare's Ear, Brown Drake, Turcks Tarantula, Kosciuszko Dun.***

Wet fly method:

• **Floating line,** 6-9 ft leader, no tippet. Sinktip/sinking line 3-6 ft leader, no tippet.

In deeper runs, flies will need to be heavily weighted to get them down quickly.

Flies:

Size 6-14 ***Sloane's Fur Fly, Rabbit Fly, Marabou Muddler, Fuzzy Wuzzy, Woolly Bugger, Matukas, Woolly Worm, Muddler Minnow, Zonker.***

POOLS

Slow moving pools form the deepest sections of a stream. The three principal parts of a pool are the headwater, body and tailout. The headwaters and tailouts of most pools provide a good habitat for **mayfly nymphs, stonefly nymphs** and **caddis nymphs** and regularly hold the best fish. Small **freshwater crays** are also taken by trout at times.

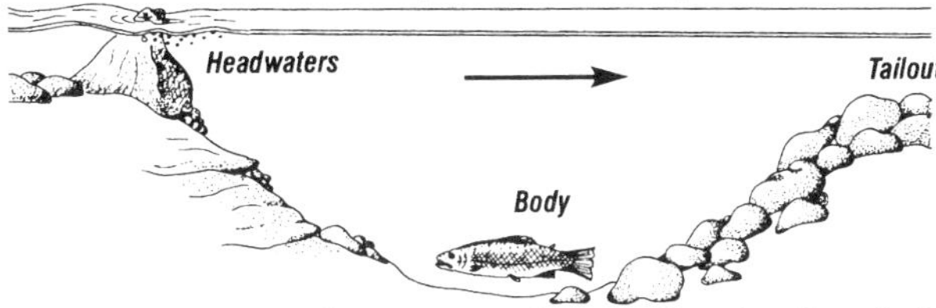

Prime features include:

- Headwaters, particularly the eyes
- Overhanging trees & foliage
- Seams • Stream bed • Tailout

Feeding habits:

- Trout in the headwaters are usually aggressive, opportunistic feeders.
- Larger fish rarely venture to the surface in daylight but will often feed in the tailout during low light conditions at dawn & dusk.

Nymphing methods:

• **Floating line,** 9 ft leader, 2-3 ft 5x tippet.

• **Sinktip line,** 6 ft 3x tippet. Best option in dirty water.

• **Floating line with indicator** and weighted nymph, 12 ft leader, 4x tippet. Best in clear water and when polaroiding.

Flies:

Size 6-14 ***Pheasant Tail Nymphs, Seals Fur Nymphs, Gray or Red Squirrel Nymphs, Hare & Copper, Zug Bug, Philo Thorax, Teeny Nymph, Tellico, Bird's Nest, Fledermaus.***

Wet fly methods:

• **Sinktip/sinking line,** 3-4 ft leader, no tippet.

Ensure you fish on or near the bottom with varied retrieves i.e. slow, dead slow, moderate or quick. Weighted patterns or split shot directly above the fly will help it sink.

Flies:

Size 6-14 ***Marabou Muddler, Tom Jones, Craig's Nigh-time, Fuzzy Wuzzy, Black & Peacock Spider, Woolly Bugger, Picket Pin, Janssens Minnows.***

Dry fly methods:

• **Floating line,** 9-15 ft leader, 2-4 ft 5x, 6x tippet.

In deep pools dry fly action can be limited, but big fish will come up to the dry in clear water. On warm, windy summer days terrestrial patterns may be productive.

Flies:

Size 10-12-14 ***Red Tag, Coch-y-Bondhu, Bogong Moth, Zulu, Twilight Beauty, Tup's Indispensable, Blue Dun, Greenwell's Glory, Turnbull's Hairwing Coachman.***

FLATS

Productive flats are typically smooth, slow flowing, uniform stretches of a stream 1-4 feet deep that can sometimes resemble small lakes. Mild currents, clear water and sunlight penetration stimulate substantial weed beds that form prime habitat for **mayfly nymphs, case building caddis larvae, scuds, waterboatmen, snails** and **shrimp.** Terrestrials such as **beetles, ants** and **grasshoppers** are also taken if available.

Feeding habits:

- Trout tend to be easily spooked, highly selective, hatch driven feeders.
- Sipping rises are typical of larger fish.

Nymphing methods:

• **Floating line,** 10-12 ft leader, 2-4 ft 5x, 6x tippet.

Effective nymphing to feeding fish is very demanding. If possible, fish from a position above the trout and instigate a Parachute Cast to cover the fish.

Flies:

Size 10-16 ***Pheasant Tail Nymph, Seals Fur Nymphs, Hare & Copper, Backswimmer Nymph, Bloodworm, Black and Peacock, Hair Leg Scud.***

Dry fly methods:

• **Floating line,** 10-15 ft leader, 2-4 ft 5x, 6x tippet.

A stealthy approach and a delicate presentation of the 'right' imitation is usually mandatory. Fish will often be cruising, so polarising techniques should be adopted.

Flies:

Size 10-12-14 ***Greenwell's Glory, Dad's Favourite, Blue Wing Olive, Trico Dun, Quill Gordon, March Brown, Pale Morning Dun, Griffiths Gnat, Chuck Caddis.***

BACKWATERS / FLOODPLAINS

These occur when rivers flood over grassland and timbered areas. Fishing is generally best during the first 2 or 3 days after flooding, after time plants rot and the terrestrial food source is exhausted. Brown trout, in particular, will cruise in the shallows and feed in these areas during low light conditions. Foods include **worms, beetles, spiders** and other drowned terrestrials.

Tip: Large, contrasting wet or dry flies may be useful to attract the attention of fish in discoloured or turbid water.

Feeding habits:

Tailing fish are common.

Dry fly method:

- **Floating line,** 9-12 ft leader, 2-3 ft 4x tippet.

Avoid constant movement along the bank because this tends to spook fish. It is usually best to take up a position near prime water and wait for a fish to cruise by. Fish will often betray their location with swirls or rises. If fish are cruising in close to the bank, you may only need to dangle the fly in the water or leave it dead drift with an occasional twitch.

Flies:

Size 10-14 ***Red Tag, Coch-y-Bondhu, Humpy, Foam Beetles, Bogong Moth, Zulu, Foam Caterpillar, Inchworm, Crowe Beetle.***

Wet Fly methods:

- **Floating line,** 6-12 ft leader, no tippet.
- **Sinktip line,** 6-7 ft leader, no tippet.

Slowly strip a general purpose wet along the bottom.

Flies:

Size 8-12 ***Sloane's Fur Fly, Wigram's Robin, Mrs Simpson, Matukas, Muddler Minnow, Spuddler, Hamills Killer, Olive Leech, Lead Eye Leech, Tom Jones.***

SECTION NINE

FEEDING CLUES

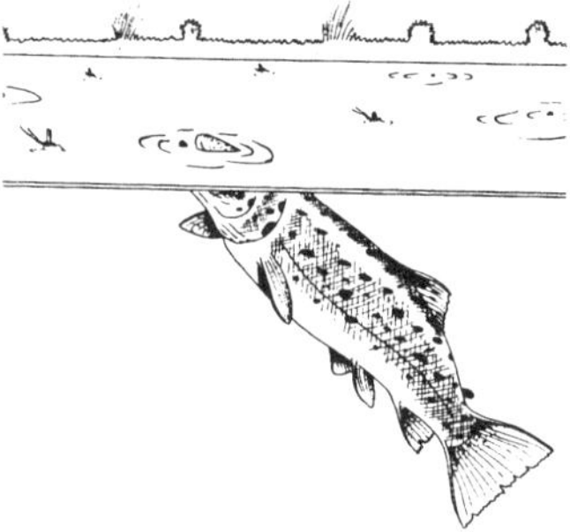

1. Normal rise with air bubbles: Indicates that trout are taking insects off the surface.

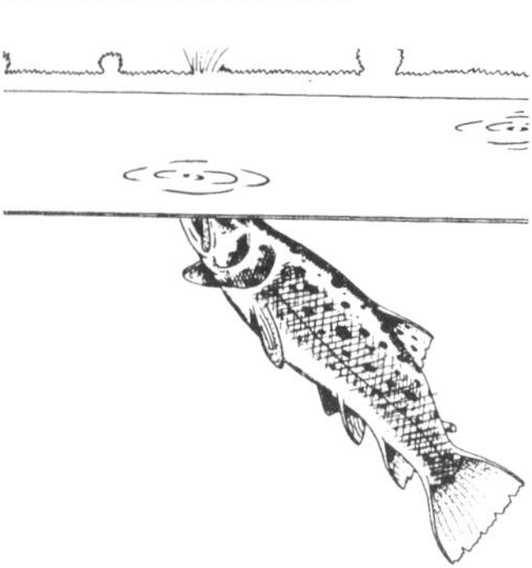

2. Normal rise without air bubbles: Indicates trout are taking emergers that are holding just under the surface.

3. Bulging: Occurs when trout that are holding just under the surface tilt upwards to take emergers.

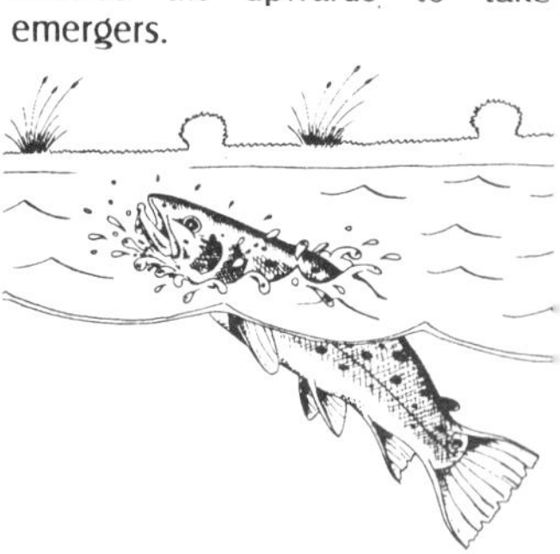

4. Splashy rise: Common in fast water when trout break the surface to feed. Hoppers and caddis pupae are also taken in this fashion.

5. Sipping rise: Trout are feeding leisurely on low riding insects e.g. beetles, ants, spent spinners.

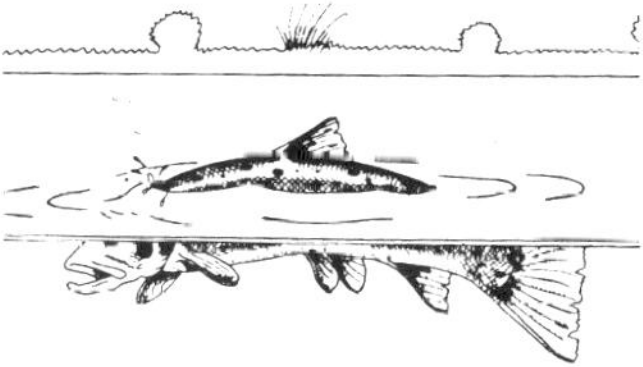

6. Porpoise rise (Head to tail): Common in flats or backwaters when trout are feeding on pupae, spent spinners, nymphs or snails.

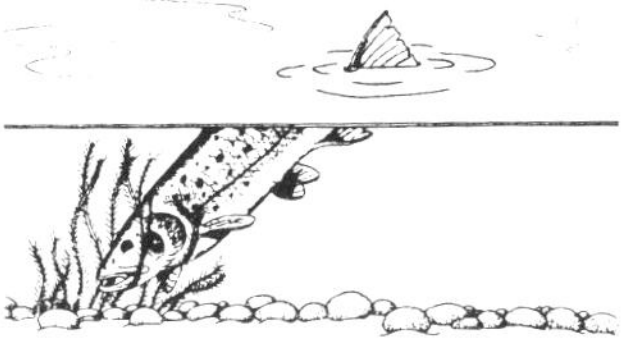

7. Tailing: This describes trout that are fossicking around on the bottom in the shallows exposing their backs, dorsal fins or tails as they rummage through weed beds for nymphs, scuds or other aquatic food items.

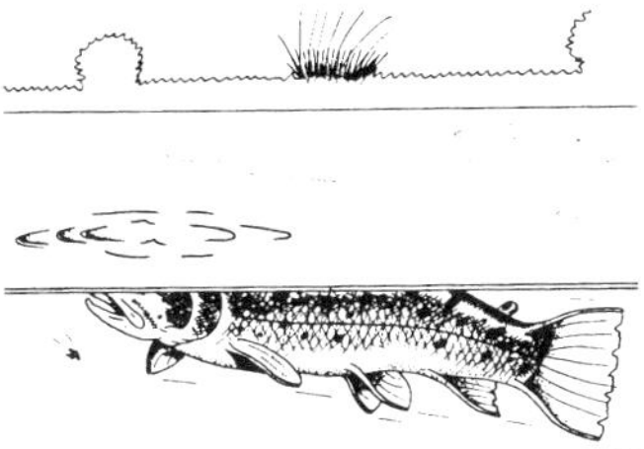

8. Boil: Indicates that trout are targeting fast moving emergers, usually caddis pupae, below the surface film.

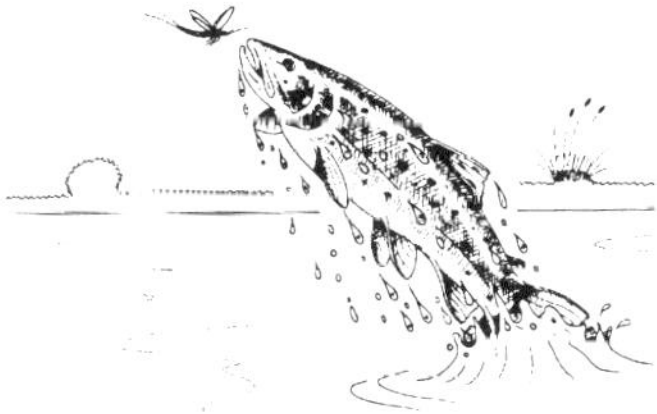

9. Leaping fish: Trout are feeding on low flying insects like adult caddis or mayfly spinners.

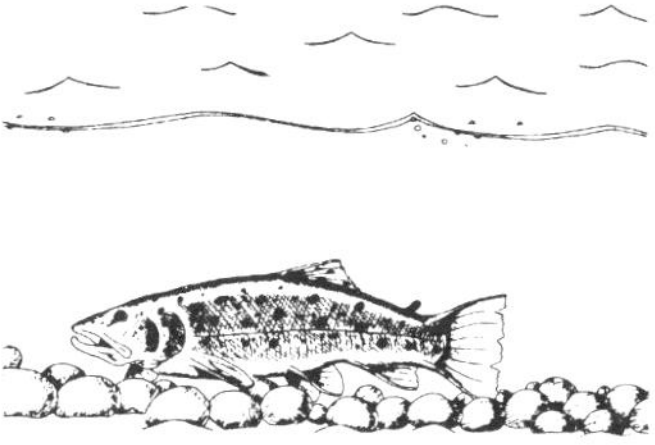

10. No indication: You are fishing blind and will need to investigate the likely food source or make an informed guess.

SECTION TEN

TROUT FOODS

MAYFLIES

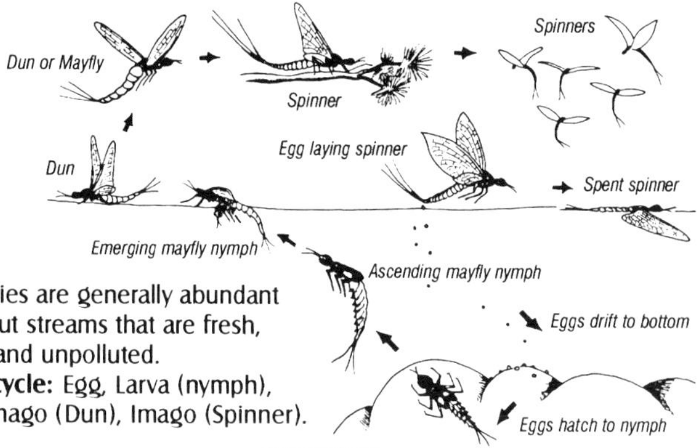

Mayflies are generally abundant in trout streams that are fresh, cool and unpolluted.
Life cycle: Egg, Larva (nymph), Subimago (Dun), Imago (Spinner).

— NYMPHS —

Nymphs primarily live and grow on the stream bed for up to 12 months feeding on decaying vegetation, plankton and algae. When they have matured they swim/float to the surface to emerge into the dun. The stop/start ascendancy makes emerging nymphs easy prey.

Where found: All water types.
Season: All year round.
Time: Anytime.

Tip: When nymphing in slow water, give the fly a twitch to draw attention to it.

Feeding patterns: Stream-bed nymphs 2, 5, 6, 10; Emerging nymphs 2, 3.

FLIES: Size 12-14-16. ***STREAM-BED NYMPHS - Seal's Fur Nymphs, Pheasant Tail Nymph, Red Fox Squirrel Nymph, Hare & Copper, Sloane's Possum Nymph, Flashback Nymphs, Sawyer Nymph, Pheasant Tail Nymph.***

FLIES: SIZE 12-14-16. ***EMERGING NYMPHS - Cul De Canard, Suspender Nymphs, Parachute Brown, Possum, Balloon Emerger, Polywing Emerger, Loop Wing Emerger.***

— DUNS —

These are the dull coloured winged insects that emerge from the nymphal shuck. They will drift with the current a short distance until their wings have dried, then fly to nearby foliage.

Season: Early spring until late autumn.

Time: Mid morning until late afternoon.

Feeding clues: 1.

FLIES: Size 12-14 ***March Brown, Hardy's Favourite, Highland Dun, Greenwell's Glory, Blue Winged Olive, Dark Cahill, Penstock Brown, Whirling Dun, Twilight Beauty, Tassie Dun, Wickham's Fancy, Kosciuszko Dun, Dad's Favourite, Blue Dun, Red Quill, Brown Drake, Pale Evening Dun.***

— SPINNERS —

'Duns' shed their exoskeleton to emerge as the often brilliantly coloured imago or 'spinner'. On dusk swarms of these graceful insects will appear over the river to mate. They then dip the surface to deposit their eggs.

Time: Dusk.

Feeding patterns: 1, 9.

FLIES: Size 12-14 ***Macquarie Red, Orange/Red or Black Spinner patterns, Macquarie Black, Twilight Beauty, Compara Spinner, Trico Spinner, Quill Gordon, Poly Wing Spinner and countless local patterns worldwide.***

— SPENT SPINNER —

After mating, females will return to the water to lay their eggs and die. The dead 'spent' spinner lies flush in the surface film with wings outspread, and often drift into backwaters where trout leisurely mop them up.

Time: Dusk and dawn.

Feeding patterns: 1, 5, 6.

FLIES: Size 12-14 ***Black Spent Spinner, Green Para Drake, Rusty Spinner and Parachute-hackle or Clipped-hackle patterns (Greenwell's Glory, Cocky Spinner, countless local patterns).***

Tip: Fully grease the leader and fly. Facing the setting sun and getting down low to the water will help you to spy rises in the afterglow at dusk.

CADDIS

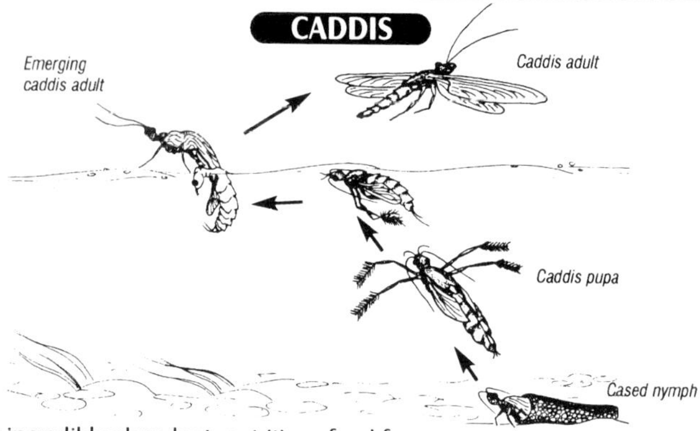

An incredibly abundant, nutritious food for trout, found in most parts of streams and rivers.

Life cycle: Egg, Larva (Nymph), Pupa, Adult.

— NYMPHS —

Most species resemble small caterpillars and are mainly bottom dwellers. The 3 most commonly imitated types are: i) Bottom dwelling cased caddis nymphs which build protective cases of stone and gravel around their fragile bodies. ii) Swimming stick caddis nymphs whose cases are made from twigs and plant matter. iii) Swimmer nymphs which do not build a protective case and swim freely with the current.

Where found: Weed beds and amongst stone and rocks.

Season: All year round.

Time: Anytime.

Feeding patterns: 2, 5, 6, 10.

FLIES: Size 12-14-16

Cased Caddis Nymphs: ***Bead Head Hare's Ear, Hare & Copper, Carrot Nymph, Black & Peacock, Goulburn Caddis, Brassie, Peeking Caddis, Drifting Cased Caddis.***

Stick Caddis Nymph: ***Murray Wilson Sticky Caddis, Wigram's Stick Caddis, Bailey's Stick Caddis.***

Free Swimmers: ***Goulburn Caddis, Olive Caddis Larva, Buckskin Caddis Nymph, Green Rockworm.***

— PUPA —

At a predetermined time nymphs will seal up their cases to pupate. When ready they will chew their way out of their cocoons and swim rapidly to the surface to emerge into adults. During this ascent and emergence phase the helpless pupae are avidly taken by trout.

Season: Spring to late summer.

Time: Late afternoon until dark.

Feeding patterns: 2, 3, 8, 10.

FLIES: Size 12-14-16 - ***Deep Sparkle Pupa, Emergent Sparkle Pupa, CDC Caddis Emerger, Krystal Flash Caddis Pupa, Soloman's Caddis Pupa.***

— ADULT —

Adult caddis resemble small moths and are targeted by trout as they flutter across the water surface in an attempt to become airborne or when females return to deposit eggs.

Time: Morning, afternoon and into the night.

Feeding patterns: 1, 4, 9.

FLIES: ***Elk Hair Caddis, Goddard Caddis, Turnbull's Hairwing Coachman, Irresistible Adams, Stimulator, Pye's Sedge, Green Peter, Shannon Moth, Skittering Caddis, Sparkle Caddis.***

STONEFLIES

These robust bottom dwelling nymphs form a primary food source for trout in some areas. Unlike many other aquatic insect species, the stonefly emerges by crawling out of the water on to the bank. The adult is rarely available to trout.

Life cycle: Egg, Larva (nymph), Adult.

Where found: Common beneath rocks in fast, unpolluted highly oxygenated water ie riffles, rapids.

Season: All year.

Time: Most active at dawn, dusk. Emergence generally takes place at night.

Feeding patterns: 2, 5, 6, 10.

FLIES: Size 8-10-12-14 - ***Bead Head Hare & Copper, Kaufman's Stonefly, Bird's Stonefly Nymph, Black Stone, Montana, Terrible Troth, Mono Stonefly Nymph, Morristone, Whitlock Black Stone.***

BEETLES

Beetles are common in areas where foliage hangs over the water. Flying species often get blown on to the water offering trout a large, easily taken bite.
Where found: Along banks with over hanging trees and foliage.
Season: Summer.
Time: Best when windy on warm days.
Feeding patterns: 1, 2, 5.

FLIES: ***Red Tag, Coch-y-Bondhu, Geehi Beetle, Black and Brown Beetle patterns, Great Lake Beetle, Ti Tree Beetle, Foam Beetle patterns, Jassid, Green Leaf Hopper, Red Palmer.***

HOPPERS

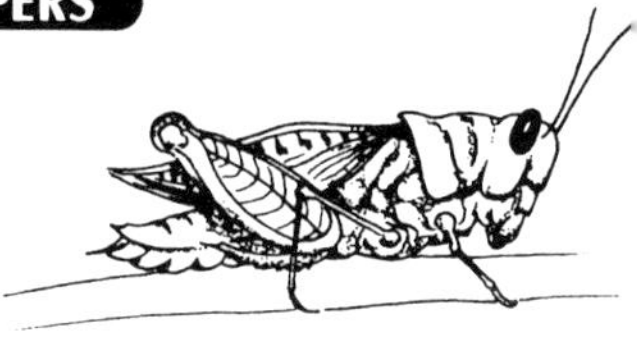

These insects are prolific in summer and often get blown or fall onto the water and are keenly taken by trout.
Life cycle: The female lays her eggs before winter, they hatch in spring and reach maturity in summer.
Where found: Bankside grasses.
Season: Mid summer to autumn.
Time: Late morning until late afternoon on fine, warm, sunny days. Best when windy.
Feeding patterns: 4.

FLIES: ***Nobby Hopper, Berchdolt, Glen Innes Hopper, Snowy Mountains Hopper, Muddler Hopper, Joe's Hopper, Daves Hopper, Letort Hopper, Whit's Hopper.***

ANTS

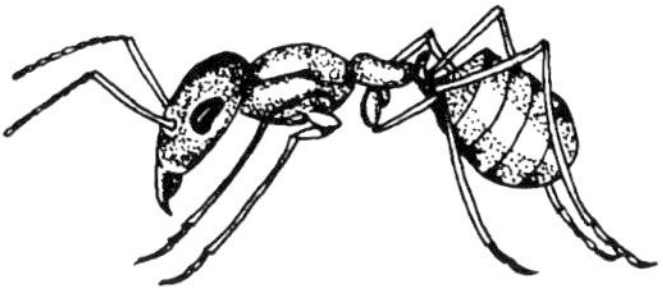

In some areas, ants are choice food items and can produce intense feeding and spectacular fishing.

Life cycle: Occasionally the mating cycle sees ant colonies take to the air in huge swarms over the water. Once mating is completed the male ants fall to the water, often in their thousands, to die and the trout will gorge themselves. At other times trout simply take hapless ants that have fallen or been blown from overhanging foliage or the bank.

Where found: Dead trees and piles of rotting timber are prime locations.

Season: Most active in spring through summer.

Time: Not critical but warm or humid days can increase ant activity.

Feeding patterns: 1, 2, 5.

FLIES: Size 12-20 ***Hard Bodied Black Ant, Black Para Ant, Red Fur Flying Ant, E-Z Sight Ant, Black/Red & Grey Ant, Magic Wing Flying Ant, Red McMurray Ant, Rod's Black Ant, Carpenter Ant, Black Deer Hair Ant.***

SNAILS

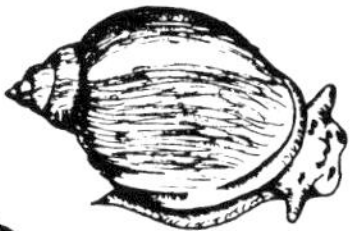

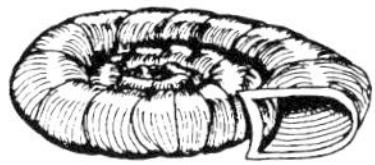

Snails slowly crawl about the weeds feeding on algae and decaying vegetation.

Where found: Weed beds in slow flowing rivers, flats and backwaters.

Season: All year.

Time: Anytime.

Feeding patterns: 4, 6, 7, 10.

FLIES: ***Black & Peacock, Coch-y-Bondhu, Red Tag, Super Snail, Snail Fly, Floating Snail, Taylor Snail, Peacock Snail.***

Tip: Dead drift snail patterns after water turbulence from strong winds may have dislodged them from weeds. If fishing over weed beds use a strike indicator to regulate the depth of the fly so you don't get continually snagged.

SCUDS

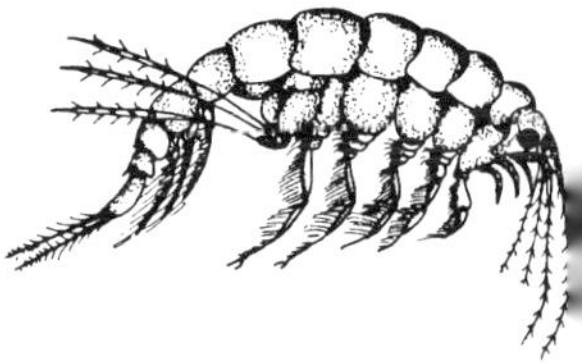

These crustaceans are active in low light conditions and are keenly taken by trout.
Where found: Weed beds in slow flowing rivers, flats and backwaters.
Season: All year.
Time: Dawn, dusk and overcast days are productive.
Feeding patterns: 7, 10.

FLIES: Size 10-14 ***Hair Leg Scud, Yellowstone Scud, Nymbeet, Seal's Fur Nymph, Hare and Copper, Ostrich Scud, Troth Scud.***

SHRIMP

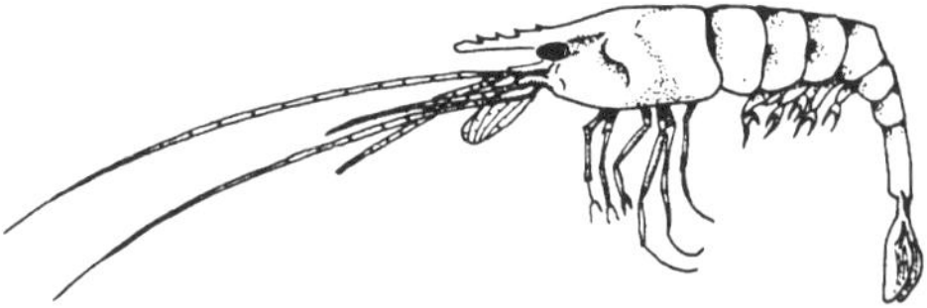

These elongate, largely transparent crustacea normally grow from 30 to 35mm in length. Breeding takes place in spring with the eggs hatching in summer.
Where found: Common amongst weed beds in flats and backwaters
Season: Spring to early autumn.
Time: Most active in low light conditions.
Feeding patterns: 7, 8, 10.

FLIES: ***Tom Jones, Clausers Crayfish, small Green Matuka, Green Nymph, Pink Shrimp, Werner Shrimp, Mysis Shrimp.***

Tip: Foraging shrimp move forward when feeding but dart backwards at speed when fleeing.